1959 Lark

Linda Hyatt Cancél

ISBN: 978-1-59849-389-4
Library of Congress Control Number: 2025917947

BISAC Codes:
BIO000000 BIOGRAPHY & AUTOBIOGRAPHY / General
BIO001000 BIOGRAPHY & AUTOBIOGRAPHY / Artists, Architects, Photographers
BIO026000 BIOGRAPHY & AUTOBIOGRAPHY / Memoirs

Printed in China

This book was printed using European Union Regulation on
Deforestation-free Products (EUDR) compliant paper.

Editor: Ruthie Little
Design: Soundview Design

Requests for such permissions should be addressed to:

Peanut Butter Publishing
206-860-4900
info@peanutbutterpublishing.com
www.peanutbutterpublishing.com

Introduction

Throughout the years when I've met new people, the subject of my sister Melissa's illness and passing at the tender age of four and a half years has come up naturally in conversation or has been shared on a need-to-know basis. Childhood friends would be subjected to a walk to the cemetery to be "introduced" to my beloved and sorely missed little sister. To know and understand me as a person, and as an artist, meant one may have to hear of Melissa's short, angelic life.

There were many times I wondered why losing her had to happen, despite knowing that even to this day, with all the advancements of modern medicine, there is absolutely no cure for or control over her devastating cancer diagnosis. Why us? Why our family? My father once asked, "Why not us?" Those words from him brought me a measure of healing, knowing that acceptance had graced his heart. As a young mother with small children of my own, my father tearfully said to me, "Linda, it's okay for you to talk about Melissa...I want to talk about her." It was heart-shattering. For the first time, I realized that in an effort to protect my parents from more sad reminders of a parent's worst nightmare, I hadn't spoken of her or my feelings about her passing to them.

As I matured and gained new experiences, my feelings of isolation and trauma slowly began to subside with the understanding that everyone inevitably has suffered or will suffer, carry burdens, endure hardship, and hopefully will be refined as pure gold from their personal crucibles.

The need to write my family's story would become increasingly clearer when a new Santa Cliff Snider painting was completed and reproduced as a fine art print. The artists were invited to premiere their work in the Remarque Gallery's booth at the Holiday Market in the Greensboro Coliseum in North Carolina. From year to year, I would try to remember as many faces and names as possible of returning collectors, and it would warm my heart as we smiled and recognized one another. The interest in the story of what inspired each painting took the dialogue to deeper levels, as people shared their joys and, sometimes tearfully, their heartbreaks with the artist, and what the image meant to them personally. To know that the art was given as a gift, whether it was for Christmas, housewarming, or to welcome a new baby, meant so much to me.

When I found myself sharing the same stories, reciting them again and again...the loop that has played over and over in my mind since childhood...I knew I must write, if not for myself and others, then for a precious little girl whose memory I will not allow to be forgotten. With a gentle mandate from Santa Claus himself, "You have to write this story. How can you not?"

Acknowledgments

This book is dedicated to my loving parents, John and Phyllis Hyatt.

My sister: Melissa Ann Hyatt

My children: Philip, Stephen, Maria and Phillip, John and Morgan, Telma and Kery, Maris, and all the grandchildren thus far and in the future…

My grandparents:
Paul W. and Melissa McCollum Hyatt
Byron S. and Pansy Farance Kisamore

My friends and oil painting teacher: William and Marguerite Pogue

Thank you to my loving husband, soulmate, and partner: John Sebastian Marrazzo

With special thanks to:
Don and Sherry Kisamore
Claude and Bettie Trowbridge
Mr. and Mrs. Robert Clifton Snider Jr.
William and Ethel Lindsey and Family
L.K. and Bev Mihalovich
Pastor and Mrs. Alvin C. Lustie
Marvin and Sally Rose
Dick and Betty Jo O'Brien
The Koschutzke Family
Gail Carey-Cormier
Tony Bailey
The Family of Maj. Richard A. and Irene Carey
Edward and Shannon Emory
Walter and Dianne Catarius
Mr. David George
Mike and Kathy Lust
Richard Willner
Mrs. Linda Terry and Family
Suzy Heath
Steve Schroeder and his Band of Merry Men
Alan Pestana

(Like to the lark at break of day arising
From sullen earth) sings hymns at heaven's gate;

—William Shakespeare
(Sonnet 29: When, in disgrace with fortune and men's eyes)

Chapter 1

The Little Hyatt Girl

I stepped out into the late August sunshine to take a break from demonstrating oil painting at the Northeast Washington Fair. There I had exhibited with 4-H and oil painted in Mr. Pogue's art class booth over forty years prior. As I was enjoying the familiar sights, smells, and warmth of the regional celebration of agricultural bounty, I saw something in the gravelly dirt and picked it up. It was a rusty metal washer. The other volunteers and I had just been discussing the mystery of life and how things seem to come full circle, so I put the talisman in my pocket.

A few weeks before, my mother had passed away after an intense struggle with congestive heart failure. I had returned home ten months earlier to help with her medical decisions and a difficult transition from her beloved homeplace to nursing home facilities. She had prepared well, but there was still the unpleasant task of complicated paperwork and the sad reality of a once strong and self-reliant woman who refused to accept her own frailty. And who could blame her? Only a few years before, in her mid-seventies, she could still do cartwheels and would haul, split, chop, and stack over twelve cords of wood for the winter.

I had arrived the week of Thanksgiving and there was a snowstorm the morning after what is usually my favorite holiday celebration. The days were short and dark, and there was little comfort for the future. One day at the facility where my mother was staying for therapy, a pleasant voice said, "You must be the little Hyatt girl!" At nearly fifty-five years of age, I was amused and took it as a compliment. It also occurred to me that I had been thinking to myself, "Here I am, back in my folks' house watching *Gilligan's Island*!" That endearing statement released a wave of emotions as I was staying in my parents' home, surrounded by the life they built. It was an opportunity for me to reflect, revisit, and really absorb and appreciate who they were: the most decent, hardworking, and virtuous human beings I have ever known.

Our more recent ancestors, several of whom fought in the Civil War—for both North and South—had settled the rugged river canyons of Idaho and Oregon between the 1870s and early 1900s, migrating from various states in the East and Midwest, descendants of those who all arrived on this continent before the American Revolution and also fought for our country's independence.

Dad's brother Jerome, sister Rose Marie, and my dad – late 1930s

In Idaho, on a hot summer day in 1946, three siblings and the neighborhood kids sneaked into Paul Hyatt's Buick and traveled twelve miles east from Lewiston to Spalding on a highway that snaked between steep canyons and the Clearwater River, to swim at what is now Nez Perce National Historical Park. When the latter-day Corps of Discovery returned safely to Lewiston, they all jumped out of the big car and the driver, who could barely see over the steering wheel, turned the odometer back. John Hyatt was twelve years old.

Although both my grandmothers were born and raised in the canyons above the Clearwater River, my mother's parents, because of The Great Depression, moved to Ohio for work and to be near my grandfather's family. Born there in 1935, my mother had fond memories of growing up on a small farm in Williamsfield in Ashtabula County, where her two older sisters, Aloha and Helen, and younger brother Don helped with work on the farm, played in the school band, and roamed the beauty of the fields and hardwood forests. She also spoke of the deprivation, fears, and trauma of WWII that she felt as a child; in case of attack by the enemy, her plan was to gather up her kitties and run to the barn for safety.

My mother and her younger brother Don with their pets – around 1940

My mother never missed a Cleveland Indians game. She would sit by the radio and listen for hours, imagining every play, cheering on or scolding her favorite player, Larry Doby. Their father, Byron Kisamore, was a hunting guide for Bruno Betzel, a major league baseball player, and scout for the team. Bruno gave my grandfather tickets for the family to attend a Cleveland Indians game in 1949, after the Indians' 1948 World Series win against the Boston Braves.

For the sake of aging parents, the family returned to Idaho in 1949, and my parents met and fell in love in Lewiston High School. They both had green eyes for one another and would meet at the corner of 3rd Street and 8th Avenue and hold hands on the way to school. Among their things, I found their high school rings, each resized to fit the other.

At the age of nineteen, my father volunteered for the U.S. Army draft during the Korean War. Serving in the Signal Corps, he was selected from twelve-hundred enlisted men at Fort Hood as an aide-de-camp to several major generals and their families. He was the chauffeur, maintained the house and grounds, killed rattle snakes hanging from trees in the yard, and drove their children to school.

After my parents' marriage in 1954, my mother joined my father in Killeen, Texas, arriving from Idaho on a Greyhound bus with a purse full of silver dollars. She then also became an assistant to the families, doing the cooking, cleaning, laundry, and ironing. John and Phyllis Hyatt were not yet twenty-one years of age. The war ended before his stint was over, and when the time came to return to Idaho and college life, they did so in a brand-new India Ivory/Navajo Tan 1955 two-door Chevrolet 210 Delray, having saved enough for the down payment.

To be a child of John and Phyllis Hyatt is an honor and a safe haven in which to dwell.

Phyllis and John Hyatt – circa 1955

CHAPTER 2

1959 Lark

When my father was a full-time student at the University of Idaho, he worked several part-time jobs while my mother worked full-time at a savings and loan to put him through school. The '55 Chevy was traded in for a 1959 two-door White Sand Studebaker Lark, and as I arrived ten days early on the sixteenth day of that April, Dad made his way up the steps to the nursery at Gritman Memorial Hospital in Moscow. Students from the university worked part time there washing windows, and as he walked up to the group, he saw them pointing and laughing at the babies in the bassinets. There I was—five pounds, four ounces, and seventeen inches long next to a ten-pound baby—and Dad would chuckle as he remembered that day. It made me smile to think of them all being so entertained.

My earliest memory in life is watching fireworks from the bluffs above the Snake River on the Idaho-Washington border. As an adult, I asked my mother what my age was when watching the light show from Prospect Park in a little white metal chair. She was shocked that I remembered. "Why, you were only fifteen months old!" As a landscape painter, recalling the way the air felt and how golden light, created by volcanic soil, was absorbed into skies of dark blue velvet was the beginning of a never-ending quest to capture in oils the way the atmosphere affects the horizon.

A month earlier in 1960, my father graduated with a bachelor's degree in Education, majoring in Industrial Arts and minoring in Math and History. Resumes were sent to several school districts: Calgary, Canada; Ely, Nevada; and Northport, Washington. Northport (pop. 482) called first, so our little family, our dog Ringo, and the twenty-six-foot trailer moved to a vacant lot in what is now parking for Northport High School. In my father's combination classroom of sixth and seventh graders was future acclaimed writer,

NOV 1960

Linda Lael Miller, now a *New York Times* and *USA Today* bestselling author. In an article, she credits the influence of her teachers in her hometown of Northport, noting Mr. Hyatt's encouragement of an A on her assignment and a note written across the top, telling her that she should become a writer. She writes, "Other teachers contributed, but Mr. Hyatt and my high school teacher, Crystal Harworth, were pivotal."

My mother could not resist the little black and white Spitz puppy that she had seen at a store in Moscow. Ringo was Ringo before the Beatles became a part of pop culture—he was named for the white rings around his eyes. Since he was a herding dog, he had made his presence known all over the campus at the university, looking for his charge. He would get first lick on the neighbor kids' Tootsie Roll Pops, scared the mailman, and learned a new trick almost every day. In Northport, he would make his way up the fire escape at the old brick schoolhouse to find my dad in the classroom. At the time, I wondered why Ringo would hardly ever sit still and cuddle, but rather circled... He was herding me, keeping me safe.

My favorite toy was accidentally left behind at my grandparents' in Lewiston. Knowing how much I loved my blocks, Dad made the four-hundred-and-twenty-mile round trip to bring them home. I vaguely remember my eighteen-month-old self asking my mother where Daddy went, and her answer evoked images in my mind's eye of the tail-lights of the Lark and the back of Dad's red-head, flat-top haircut traveling through the rolling hills of the Palouse on an important mission to rescue my precious belongings. The wagon of colorful wooden blocks must have been a first Christmas or birthday gift. It helped me to learn my colors before the age of two, and I enjoyed many hours creating miniature home interiors and Mondrian-esque patterns. Every piece is still here, surviving me, my four children, and many moves around the country. In the movie *Citizen Kane*, Charles Foster Kane's mysterious last word was "Rosebud." I jest that mine will be "Playskool."

What I loved most of all was riding in the front seat of the Lark, standing behind Dad's right shoulder with my arm around his neck as he carefully drove the few blocks to the post office. I just wanted to go wherever he went. The hardware store, the lumber yard to load mill ends, and even the city dump—it didn't matter. All was right with the world when he was around.

Chapter 3

Flying Wheelchair

Budget cuts at the school created an exodus of teachers to other districts, so the fall of 1961 brought a move to Kettle Falls, Washington, into a little log house at the corner of 7th and Kalmia Street—and a few minutes after midnight on Christmas Eve, a precious baby sister, Melissa Ann. The blond-haired, hazel-eyed angel was named after my father's mother, who loved animals and admired the teachings of St. Francis of Assisi. But as far as I was concerned, Melissa belonged to me.

Her first year was happy and healthy. At about the age of eighteen months, Melissa began having health problems, and the doctors could not find a definitive diagnosis. Adding to our parents' fear and frustration was that they were told that she was just a fretful child. My mother insisted something was wrong, and after many exhausting trips to doctors around the state, physicians at the University of Washington Hospital finally detected a spinal cord astrocytoma: a rare, invasive, star-shaped cancer cell that had been causing Melissa great pain and discomfort.

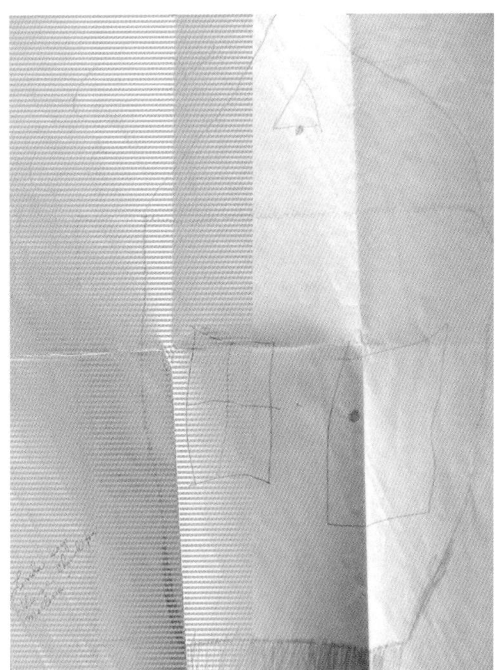

When I was five years old, the Sunday school teacher wrote this note for my parents on my drawing: "Linda says this is a church for Melissa"

On one visit to a hospital in Spokane, I was to stay outside of the examining room. Two sets of double doors were propped open in the long corridor so that I could be seen from where I was sitting at the end of the hallway. Our mother, the doctor, and his assistants were backlit by the morning sun as my sister cried. Her screams echoed down the industrial pale-green painted hallway and bounced and shattered into acid-yellow shards of sound. Through the years, I have often thought of that day—no matter how painful—and what strikes me most and the feeling that I am left with, is that those double doors were left open so that I would not be alone.

When she was about three years old, the physicians in Seattle attempted to alleviate Melissa of her pain. Although inoperable, an eight-inch incision was made in her back, and the draining of the cyst gave her a reasonably pain-free few months. During her recovery at the hospital, the nurses and our mother asked if I would like to take Melissa for a walk around the halls in her wheelchair. I was thrilled to be bestowed such a great responsibility and to be doing something for and with her. We made our way to the end of the hallway and took a left at the corner. Before us was a hallway the length of the building, and I yelled, "Let's RUN!" I could barely see over the top of the wheelchair and ran as fast as I could, and Melissa needed no encouragement to shout, "BEEP BEEP! BEEP BEEP!" We were laughing wildly as people scrambled to get out of our way. We were finally detained at the nurses' station and escorted back to her room.

Linda - age 6

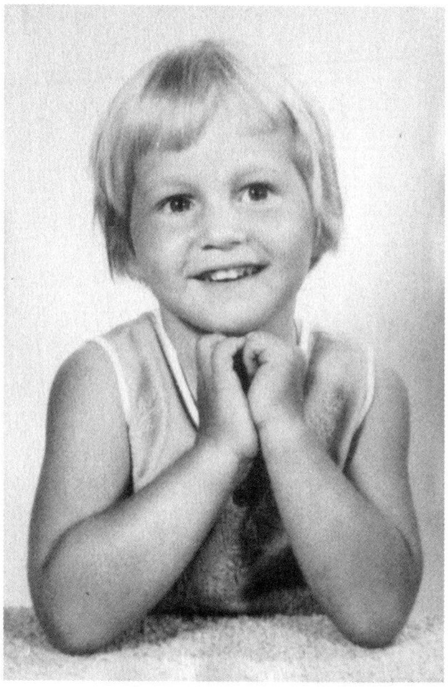

Melissa - age 3 ½

It was a happy and carefree summer; we ran and played, dressed our cats in doll clothes and took them for strolls in the baby buggy, tried to dig to China from the driveway, which became too laborious, so we switched to being pirates with buried treasure, hid under the bridal veil bushes carpeted beneath with violets, and shared a popsicle on car rides. The clippings from the lawnmower were gathered and formed into nests in the yard, where we watched and waited for homeless birds to lay their eggs. Our mother's parents, Byron and Pansy Kisamore, delivered a green swing set that Grandpa had welded from pipe and parts and pieces of discarded sets. He also crafted a wooden doll bed for which Grandma Pansy sewed little embroidered sheets, pillowcases, and a bedspread. We spent many joyful hours playing with those made-with-love gifts. Melissa always looked to me for direction and happily went along with whatever I decided we should do.

Chapter 4

Angel Cats and Ladybugs

The autumn of 1965 arrived, and I entered the first grade. School and recess were fun, and the first word we learned to read in Mrs. Miller's class was from a poster of a girl pointing at an apple, exclaiming, "LOOK!" My dad was doing his very best to teach school, make the trips to the hospital in Seattle to be with his wife and younger daughter, and take good care of me. We joked later that the man who could fix anything could not fix a ponytail to my satisfaction, so he would send me next door with a rubber band so that Ethel Lindsey could style my hair.

There were times during the school breaks when my father had to make the long trips across the state, so it was needful for me to be left in the care of their wonderful friends and colleagues from Northport, L.K. and Bev Mihalovich. There could not have been a better community of caring people to step in and provide comfort and love while I missed my family.

Kay, as he was affectionately known, was a respected principal, teacher, and coach in the Northport school district, and proud alumnus of Gonzaga University, having played basketball for the Bulldogs and served as an assistant coach for the team. I went everywhere with Bev as she volunteered much of her time to the community and school district. What I liked most was that she let me punch down the risen bread dough in the big bowl.

During one winter stay there, the Christmas decorations were up and I noticed wrapped gifts high on a shelf. Not quite able to grasp the length of days, I wondered if Santa knew I was not at home, and would he find me in Northport on Christmas Eve? Of course, my parents and sister returned in time for Christmas, but I have never forgotten the feeling of being so lost from view.

Our family had been on the road so much that our deaf cat, Biggie White, had disappeared. A day or so later, a friend and classmate, Ron Matney, burst into the first-grade classroom and asked if our pet was missing. I ran outside and sure enough, Biggie was at the school looking for us. Students were trying to help catch him, but he grew increasingly frightened and kept running. He finally let me catch him, and Mrs. Miller was kind enough to let me keep him in the supply closet where he snoozed until the school day was over, when my dad could arrive from the high school to help me get Biggie safely home.

The school ground was where Biggie came to us in the first place. My dad was the one who rescued him and brought him into the classroom. Biggie's tail had been cut off and he was filthy and confused. Dad chuckled about being embarrassed about what the principal, Mr. David Wiks, might have been thinking as he walked by the classroom, peered in, and saw Mr. Hyatt holding the cat up in front of the eighth-grade class, as if Biggie were flying.

Throughout the rest of her life, my mother carried such guilt for those weeks that she had to be away from me. I never held any resentment, understanding that Melissa needed them. My mother told me that I had shifted into behaving as another adult and that I had never, ever been unkind to my sister. She spoke of this often, and I always tried to reassure her that I never felt any lack of love or attention, and reminded her of the gifts she gave to let me know she was thinking of me. It gave me comfort to sleep in the pretty pink flannel pajamas, read the Maurice Sendak Nutshell Library (we would laugh and shout along with Pierre when he said, "I don't care!"), or use the package of straight pins with ladybugs on the tips. Who

buys a five-year-old straight pins? I was very impressed that my mother trusted me that much. To this day, I still have one of those precious straight pins, and ladybugs in many forms have become a sign of love, visitation, and presence.

Chapter 5

Skunk with the Mumps

The autumn mornings were frosty, and the leaves on the Norway maples that our mother planted in the front yard began to turn a brilliant yellow. Sadly, the effects of the last major surgery had run its course and Melissa's cancer recurred, taking her ability to walk. She was now recliner-bound but was always cheerful and never lost her sense of fun.

Mike Matney, Linda, Ron Matney, and Melissa

Halloween was just around the corner, and kids were excited to dress up in costumes and go trick-or-treating. That year, I came down with the mumps and had to stay home, so our family friend, Maxine Matney, lent Melissa and me skunk costumes that her boys had grown out of. Throw pillows that she had sewn into the outfits for tails made for a hilarious walking experience. So, sister skunks made the best of staying home and handing out candy to the ghosts and goblins. Sometimes it takes years to appreciate God's perfect plan in even the smallest details. This was to be Melissa's last Halloween, and I am now so grateful for the circumstances that kept me home with her.

Chapter 6

Here Comes Santa Claus

In Kettle Falls, a brightly lit tree on the top of the grain elevator signaled the arrival of the holiday season. We bundled up for sledding, building snow forts, and snowball fights. With their beautiful team of horses and a sleigh worthy of Santa himself, Marvin and Sally Rose would deliver gifts to every family in town, making sure everyone was remembered at Christmas. People looked forward to gathering at the high school for basketball games where the air was thick with cheering, pep band music, and hot buttered popcorn.

Our log home in Kettle Falls, Washington

The all-school Christmas program was always memorable. The bands played and the chorus sang "Angels We Have Heard on High" and "Go Tell It on the Mountain" and other traditional tunes. The grade school performed skits about the Nativity, Santa Claus, Rudolph, and Frosty the Snowman.

The lights were lowered for the grand finale—a human Christmas tree with carolers holding flashlights, covered with colorful cellophane, always brought gasps from the audience as they sang the last beautiful song of the evening. Santa Claus would make his appearance in the spotlight with a wave and a hearty "Merry Christmas and a Happy New Year!" The lights would come back on in the gymnasium and the storage doors under the stage would open and reveal row after row of

Marvin and Sally Rose

brown paper bags filled with ribbon candy, nuts in the shell, and an orange for each student. Then came the task of trying to find our families among the crowd of townspeople and make our way outside into the cold and beautiful starlit night towards home.

When Christmas Eve arrived, we celebrated Melissa's fourth birthday with our neighbors and an angel food cake that Mom had baked. Later, as we prepared for the arrival of St. Nicholas, we listened to our Christmas record of Gene Autry singing "Here Comes Santa Claus" and Burl Ives' famous rendition of "Rudolph the Red-Nosed Reindeer." We popped corn and drank bottles of ice-cold Coca-Cola that we brought from the snowbank outside the kitchen door and tried to stay awake to hear reindeer hooves on the roof.

Chapter 7

Holding Hands and Letting Go

Life unfolded as winter melted into spring, and my sister's condition continued to deteriorate. She was again taken to the hospital in Seattle where the doctors had to break the sad news to our parents. There was nothing more they could do for Melissa. They said that it would be best for them to take her home where she could be surrounded by family and the pets she loved.

Toward the end of my mother's life, I felt the need to ask her about those times that I was not privy to. She told me that after meeting with the physicians, she and my dad went for a walk around the hospital grounds. He broke down crying and said, "I wish it was me instead of her."

They brought her home and made her comfortable on the loveseat in the living room with her blankies and stuffed animals. Our beloved kitties and dog—Zoonie, Snoop, Biggie White, and Ringo—would stay near and comfort her. Although Melissa could no longer walk, our parents bought her a new pair of shiny, red patent-leather shoes. I was so happy for her. All she could wear were bedclothes, and this was something pretty. I knelt near her, and I noticed that the soles were very shiny and black...a blank canvas. Without thinking, I made marks on the soles; I drew on them. What did I just do? I had not meant to ruin her shoes that were in perfect condition…I felt so ashamed, I never told anyone, and stings of regret followed even years later.

On April 16, 1966, Mom baked a cake, we dressed up, and she created a nice little party on the folding table next to the loveseat so we could all be together to celebrate my seventh birthday.

It must have been a few days after this that Dad said to me, "Linda, let's go for a walk." We held hands and said nothing as we walked. His gait was hard to keep up with, so I walked and skipped along as fast as I could. We walked more slowly as we approached the cemetery, still holding hands. I will never forget the way the late afternoon sun sparkled through the trees in the cemetery.

Years later, I would realize that Melissa's time on Earth had been drawing near, and that my father was searching for a family resting place. Maybe we didn't drive to the cemetery because it was so close, or maybe it was because he did not want anyone to see our family car there. I wonder if walking and holding his daughter's hand was helping him to let go of another.

A few days later, on April 25th, a family friend came to get me at school and took me to Bill and Ethel Lindsey's house, and I kept asking to go home to change into play clothes. After a while, my parents drove up and I rode away between them in the front seat. The 1964 Silver Blue Chevrolet Impala station wagon traveled over the bridge at Lake Roosevelt and then up to the mountains of Sherman Pass. I turned around and saw that the little recliner was empty and asked where Melissa was. My mother's soft reply was "In Heaven." Thinking she might be teasing, I smiled nervously and asked again. For the second time, she said, "In Heaven," and then I wept.

CHAPTER 8

Red Shoes, Blue Birds, and Pink Trees

In the days before grief counseling became commonplace, my parents instinctively understood to include me in my sister's funeral arrangements. My mother selected a magenta velvet dress, sewn by her own mother, and the red patent-leather shoes for Dad and me to deliver to the funeral home. The kind director met us in the lobby, and my dad handed him the hanger with the little dress that matched mine at home, and a brown paper bag that held the shoes.

The pink dogwood

We went every day before the funeral to say our goodbyes. She looked as if she was just sleeping, so beautiful and free from pain. Years later my mother told me, at the very end, that she and my father were telling Melissa that it was all right for her to go to God.

We went to buy a memorial for the cemetery, and I was allowed to make the selection of a white marble stone. Angels unaware, Melissa had once said that she wanted a bluebird to sit on her headstone. At the kitchen table, my father designed the lettering for the stone with a blond angel baby in the top corner, "Our Christmas Angel," and in the lower right corner, a bluebird releasing its song toward heaven.

A pink dogwood tree was planted at her place in the cemetery, purchased with the nine dollars and thirty-seven cents left in her elephant bank. The winter of 1968 and 1969 was a particularly harsh one with deep snow, but my mother managed to keep the little tree alive, and every May around Memorial Day, it stands as a beacon in the back of the cemetery.

For years I carried guilt about ruining Melissa's beautiful red shoes. It was not until I began writing, and a tearful phone call to my best friend Gail, that I realized that I had sent Melissa to heaven with art, even if it was on the soles of her shoes. Sobbing, I said, "Is this the sort of thing you write about?" Always wise, comforting, and kind, Gail said, "Of course! They're like Louboutins!"

Chapter 9

Shifting Gears

That spring and summer I was my daddy's shadow. His position as the high school woodshop and graphics teacher allowed me to dig through the wood-scrap bin and find interesting pieces to hammer and nail together and draw on reams of paper to my heart's content. The tools and instruments for mechanical drawing were endlessly fascinating. I pored over his world history textbooks and marveled at the photographs of paintings and sculptures of historical figures.

Hiking in red shoes on Gold Hill with our friends and neighbors, Randy Lindsey and Gary Lindsey, above the town of Kettle Falls

Forever the driver's education instructor, he taught me to shift gears in the 1956 Golden Glow Ford truck. I would sit next to him and he would press the clutch and say, "Okay, shift into second!... Now third!... Now fourth!" Reverse was just too difficult. We drove to fire lookouts with friends and hiked on Gold Hill, where I learned to shoot the 9mm pistol.

Not long after my sister's passing, my father was elected president of the Meyers Falls Cemetery Association. He designed and routed lettering on the wooden sign he built for the entrance, located unmarked graves, and with the help of Mr. Walt Tibert, made sure that each unknown person had a concrete and metal marker. My first job was picking up aluminum foil-wrapped coffee cans of dead flowers after Memorial Day for a penny a can, and a few years later, I helped with clipping and mowing and assisted him in surveying the new section for the cemetery.

When people making funeral arrangements for their loved ones came to the house to select a burial plot, we would go outside or to another place in the house and remain quiet and respectful, while my father would unroll the map of the cemetery on the kitchen table. The saddest thing I remember from that time was a young couple whose baby had passed away. Little was said, but I knew my dad's tender heart sympathized with them and their heartbreaking loss.

As summer took a bow to autumn, we were all very excited for a baby expected in the fall. On November 11, 1966, my brother Donald James was born, named for my mother's brother and my dad's brother, both of whom were serving in the United States military... A Veterans' Day baby!

In the next few years, with a reverent acceptance, life began picking up momentum. Dad had heard of a 1935 Ford three-window coupe in an old shed on Cedar Loop outside of Colville. Mom could tell that he desperately wanted the old car because he had already approached the owners about purchasing it. He explained to his wife that he had to have the Light Gunmetal Gray car with the Bright Apple Green stripe and hubcaps because it was the same model year as her. How could she possibly refuse?

Chapter 10

Marvelous Habit-Forming Cookies

Linda and Samantha

Pleasant Sunday mornings with sunshine and soft breezes—there was hardly a soul in sight in the sleepy town of nine hundred and twenty-something residents. My new shepherd-mix rescue dog, Samantha, and I would walk together to attend Sunday school at the little community church, which had been moved to its present location from the old townsite of Kettle Falls when the Columbia River was flooded to form Lake Roosevelt.

A few blocks from our house, Samantha's owners had moved away, leaving her tied up without food or water. My mother tried to find out if they were coming back for her but to no avail, so Mom took matters into her own hands and brought Samantha home to live with us, daring anyone to arrive and try to claim my new best friend.

Every week our teacher, Marvel Boyd, would take attendance and read us an allegorical story about birds. She loved all of God's creatures, so Samantha was allowed to stay at my feet in the gathering room. Marvel was a very special person; she was of Native American descent and dedicated her life to one of service to others. She and her husband would travel with their Airstream trailer to remote areas of Mexico to minister and deliver clothing and blankets made by the women of the church. Marvel, Beth Brown, and Rose Clemons were friends, neighbors, and members of the church that I looked to with great respect as wonderful, angelic human beings. I think of them fondly as being the Three Graces of my childhood.

Marvel sometimes drove the Sunday school students to the nursing homes so that we could sing for the residents. On one occasion, she took us to visit the Dominican Sisters at Our Lady of the Valley Convent just outside of Kettle Falls. Many of the nuns there had arrived in the 1930s from Germany as young women, escaping the rise of the Third Reich. With the Colville River flowing just below, the convent grounds were serene and peaceful. It was a working farm with livestock, vegetable gardens, orchards, a gymnasium, and statuary. As we gathered in the music room, the kind Sisters served us punch and the most delicious cookies I had ever tasted.

To Highlands

The amenities at the convent would be all that a nine-year-old girl could ever want, so I told my mother that I thought I would become a nun. Her response to me was, "First of all, you are not Catholic. And second, you will not be allowed to kiss boys."

Many years later, I painted a landscape of the highlands above the convent, with the buildings hidden by the tree line above the river, and a wheat field in the foreground. The gallery owners representing my art were working with a decorator to select paintings for a multimillion-dollar retirement community in Greenville, South Carolina. The decorator looked at that particular painting and said, "Why did you bring that ugly brown thing?" It was placed over the mantel in the elegant formal dining room. The clouds must have opened and the angels sang, because that is where it stayed. I explained to the owners that the painting was not about brown, barren hills or a field and trees—it was about visiting retirement homes, nuns, and really good cookies. They smiled and said that they would never part with that painting.

Chapter II

Navigating the Waters

The next few years flowed into more of a gentle routine through the restorative qualities of the beauty of water and landscapes. In the spring of 1969, with snow still on the ground, we traveled to Arizona for an Easter visit with my father's grandmother and her sister. The sun was setting over Monument Valley as the jet descended into Phoenix, and outside the terminal the atmosphere was heavily perfumed with the intoxicating fragrance of orange blossoms.

During our stay we took the required trips to the Grand Canyon, Montezuma Castle, the Heard Museum, and other destinations of interest. As we drove by the Arizona State Capitol building, Dad pointed out the memorial statue of WWI hero and fighter ace, Frank Luke Jr., the first airman to receive the Medal of Honor. He told us that his father, as a teenager, was airman Luke's Latin tutor.

Being raised in the alpine forests and glacier valleys of the Inland Pacific Northwest, the Desert Southwest was a veritable wonderland and to swim outdoors in April was paradise.

Meanwhile, back home in Kettle Falls, in the area now known as Lake Roosevelt National Recreation Area, maintenance on Grand Coulee Dam required the lowering of the lake to levels not seen in years since the dam's construction in the 1930s by the Works Progress Administration. One hundred and thirty miles of the mighty Columbia River, known to the Native people as Nch'i-Wána was flooded to the United States/Canada border. At that time, ancient burial, hunting, and fishing grounds were desecrated, and homes and businesses were moved to higher ground. For the younger generation it was a rare glimpse into the historical significance of the area. After many years under water, the charcoal remnants of campfires could still be seen near the falls where the Indigenous peoples had fished for salmon. The kettles for which the nearby town was named were deeply carved pots in the great rocks, created by thousands of years of the force of stones in swirling water. These experiences opened up a whole new level of consciousness and appreciation for the original inhabitants of the land. I even envisioned a career as an archaeologist, but I was not gifted at science or math. I was more interested in their craftsmanship, which melded utility, function, and artistry with spiritual purpose.

Trips to visit grandparents took us to the edge of the Palouse in Southeast Washington and the great vistas of the Lewis-Clark Valley in Idaho, where the Clearwater River flows into the Snake River at the barren hills and basalt gates of Hells Canyon. They lived a half-block from Lewis and Clark State College where the Tudor revival architecture seemed reminiscent of a fairy tale setting. My grandmother Melissa, a teacher and Latin Honorary, would allow my cousins and I to purchase prom dresses from the thrift store for a few dollars. We would don our frothy ball gowns and descend the steps to the courts of tennis in our finery, and whirl and twirl and dance to our hearts' content.

Judge Paul W. Hyatt

The Nez Perce County courthouse, where my grandfather retired as District Court Judge, is also a magnificent building with a statue of a Native warrior on his horse, raising his arms to the Great Spirit. My grandfather, known as "the cowboy judge," had also served as an Idaho Supreme Court Justice and President of the Idaho State Bar Association. In a region where the Native people's history and culture was disappearing and marginalized, he was respected and known by the tribes to be fair to all.

Upon our arrival, Grandpa Hyatt would always inquire as to how my classmates and I were behaving at school. As we were seated across from each other in the living room, he gave me his full attention, and as earnestly and accurately as possible, I apprised Judge Paul Winniford Hyatt of the latest events and disciplinary action in the classroom of third-graders.

After only eight months of retirement, at the age of seventy, Grandpa passed away in 1971. At the memorial, colleagues spoke of "a true westerner, who judged a man by what he was, not by who he was"; "He used common sense and reasonableness in interpreting questions arising in a profession filled with abstractions"; "His abilities as an attorney and a judge are a matter of record"; "His inner self was one true and genteel character."

The Methodist minister who presided at the funeral was Korean and at some time in his life had been tortured, his hands missing fingers. As we paid our final respects, the minister, Reverend Joseph C.W. Lee, embraced the grief-stricken grandchildren one by one. I was concerned about mussing his spotless white robe with our tears, but all that he exuded was kindness, love, and comfort for the broken-hearted.

In her youth, from Big Canyon into Orofino, Grandma had ridden a horse to school. She had never learned to drive but preferred to walk everywhere, so their 1967 Grecian White Cadillac Sedan DeVille was gifted to my father. As much as my parents appreciated the fine automobile, they were concerned that they could not even afford new tires for it on a teacher's salary. However, we did sail toward home through the waves of wheat in the Palouse, and not too long after, in what felt like a cruise liner, it carried us to the Washington coast where a beautiful July sunset welcomed me to my first breathtaking view of the Pacific Ocean.

The weaving of experiences and images from this epoch of time undoubtedly informed the trajectory of my life.

Pansy and Byron – late 1920s – Clearwater County, Idaho

Paul and Melissa (Millie) – late 1920s – Clearwater County, Idaho

CHAPTER 12

Twelve

Twelve. The neighborhood was teeming with adolescents. Summer days and evenings were filled with swimming at the local pool, including early morning lifesaving lessons. We hiked and rode our bikes everywhere. Babysitting jobs were abundant, and many times I was so booked that I had to turn down work. Pleasant days were spent at the library, Girl Scout camp, and church youth group, and during the school year there was homework, 4-H, and sports.

Marguerite and William F. Pogue

For my mother to ask if I wanted to learn to oil paint felt like a bolt from the blue. Where? How? Paint-by-number sets were frustrating. There was a couple who had retired to the Kettle Falls area who were offering weekly oil painting classes in the room behind Clem's appliance store on the main street. Unbeknownst to me, my mother had phoned Mr. William F. Pogue to inquire if he would consider teaching a twelve-year-old. He was hesitant but agreed. She obtained the list of supplies, and we drove the seven miles to Dodson's paint store in Colville where Mrs. Dodson kindly helped us select the little tubes of Grumbacher oil paint, palette, canvas pad, and the bristle brushes I needed to begin with. On a Tuesday evening in September, I carried a plastic container filled with the precious cargo to my first class.

I was nervous and excited, but I had always felt more comfortable in the company of adults. Mr. Pogue was about the same age as my grandparents and just as kind and gentle as they. Our mild-mannered instructor patiently taught us how to arrange the colors on the palette for the greatest efficiency, and how to use a palette knife to mix the oils. A great colorist, he taught us which pigments worked together to create the realistic appearance of pine forests, clouds, and a "buttermilk" sky. A blue sky is not the blue from a tube, but a mix of Cobalt Blue, Cadmium Red, Cadmium Yellow, and Titanium White in various measures—for western skies anyway, and he would demonstrate brush strokes to achieve the desired effect. We were taught to paint what we actually saw instead of what we thought we knew, and the tonalism of distance and perspective in a landscape was a revelation. Mr. Pogue was of the generation that had to "make do," so great care was taken to clean our brushes properly in order to make them last as long as possible.

The process was mesmerizing, and I can still recall the feeling of exhilaration of producing the appearance of form, light, and shadow. One evening, after about four lessons, I carried my first finished painting home and walked into the living room where my dad was resting in his recliner. I held up the work and the lever of the footrest snapped down; he sat bolt upright looking shocked, and truly excited. It was a dusty southwest scene that I copied from a Robert Wood book provided in art class. The next week he drove me to class, walked in with a tape measure, and politely asked to take measurements of another student's wooden paint box. With only a few figures jotted down, he created a box as nice as any purchased from a store, still an absolute treasure.

Twelve. It was a good age to have something so profound become hardwired into a young person's consciousness. The fragrance of linseed oil had seeped into my heart and soul.

Chapter 13

Art and Pie Heaven

Home, church youth group, and painting class were my sanctuaries. Always one of the smallest kids in my grade, it took me off guard when someone referenced my short stature. It wasn't how I thought of myself. In art class, male, female, young and old, we were all there for one purpose—to take joy in learning a new skill in an encouraging environment. What were the chances that a highly respected businessperson with vast artistic experience would move to our little town and teach painting for two dollars and fifty cents per lesson?

I found class discussions about the Golden Age of Illustration especially fascinating. The names of Pyle, Parrish, Rockwell, and the Wyeth family dynasty gave familiarity to my great grandmother's scrapbooks rescued from the trash bin years before. As a child I spent many hours perusing the vintage magazine covers glued into the pages of the heavy books.

As the class of three to five students painted, Mr. Pogue would tell of joining the Navy at age twenty, where he played trumpet in the band and orchestra on the U.S.S. Pennsylvania. When President Harding died in San Francisco, the young man from Nebraska in the Navy band played at the memorial service held in San Diego. He described the difficulties in business during the Great Depression, rationing during World War II, and rebuilding opportunities thereafter.

His experience with commercial painting, paper-hanging, and decorating at the historic Davenport Hotel in Spokane, Washington; painting airplanes at what is now Fairchild Air Force Base; as foreman of Electrical Products, the largest sign shop in Spokane; owning the Chase Sign Company making commercial signs and highway billboards; contracting with Enco, now Exxon, to maintain their signs in Washington and surrounding states; and finally as manager and salesman at Columbia Paint Company all contributed to his deepening interest in fine art and expertise in color theory. Required retirement at age sixty-five is what brought Bill and Marguerite Pogue to Kettle Falls, Washington.

Ever so humble, I am not sure that these two earth angels ever realized what they meant to those of us who were fortunate to be a part of their oeuvre. Because of their inspiration and influence on the community, the Old Mission Art Gallery was formed by them with the help of their students and interested patrons, in what is now the lobby of Woodland Theater Productions in Kettle Falls, Washington.

By eleventh grade, schoolwork, painting class, sports, and a thirty-hour work week at a local restaurant kept me very busy. The year before, every Sunday afternoon without fail, in sunshine or snow, and with the highest of standards, was spent learning to drive a stick shift in a 1968 Seafoam Green Ford truck with a black powder coat cab roof, with my own personal driver's education teacher.

In order to preserve the pristine condition of my mother's 1974 Bright Red Ford Mustang II coupe, my folks bought a 1966 Volkswagen Beetle for me to drive, the color of Sea Sand. They had recently purchased property and built a house on the north end of the Huckleberry Mountain Range, between Kettle Falls and Colville. So, on painting nights when class was dismissed, the wooden paint box would be loaded into the Bug, and my hope was that the radio would get reception from a classic rock station in Spokane. When the music and nights were clear, I followed the moon home through the beautiful dark-blue velvet landscape.

A local favorite, the D & P restaurant where I worked was well-known for the great food and the variety of homemade pies and cheesecakes in the large display case at the entry. What enthralled me even more was the sophisticated décor—mid-century modern with white Eames-style tables and chairs. The owner, Mr. Donald Baker, a world class artist, created the large batik of a medieval king that filled the center of one wall under the vaulted ceiling. Flanking this magnificent, elegantly framed piece were large pen and inks of the apostles John and Paul. I could not believe my good fortune. This was art and pie heaven!

John Hyatt – first solo flight on August 22, 1979

As time permitted, my father worked to restore the 1935 coupe and hated to part with it when the move to the mountain homesite provided no place for adequate storage. His expertise and craftsmanship were then transferred to the cabinetry, built-ins, and trim moldings in our new house that he designed. When all things pertaining to priorities of family, work, and home were in order, my father began pursuing his lifelong dream, his own slice of heaven: flying lessons and obtaining his pilot's license.

Chapter 14

Your Daughter Is a Dreamer

My French teacher once said to her colleague, "John, your daughter is a dreamer." He did not appear disappointed when he mentioned their conversation to me. In fact, I detected a bit of pride. Having always felt deficient in math, music, and science, I did my best to maintain decent grades in those subjects, but I struggled as though they were a foreign language. History, English, vocabulary, and grammar were a piece of cake, and I devoured those areas of study. I did not want to sit in a classroom learning French, but rather travel to Paris, the City of Lights...

...And travel there I did. Understanding my aspirations for art and painting, my parents sacrificed so that I could travel with my father to the British Isles and France. To behold Leonardo's Burlington House Cartoon of The Virgin and Child with St. Anne and St. John the Baptist at the National Gallery in London was otherworldly. Jacques-Louis David's powerful neo-classical works in the Salle Daru and the Winged Victory of Samothrace up the Escalier Daru in the Denon Wing of the Louvre would have been plenteous...but to gaze upon Leonardo's masterpiece, the Mona Lisa, was a transcendent and spiritual experience.

The walk from the Louvre to the Eiffel Tower was a lot further than it looked, so I was thankful for the cute, comfortable walking shoes to wear for my sojourn, perhaps subconsciously selected, which happened to be red. When we finally arrived at the Eiffel Tower it started to rain, so I inquired of the tall, dark, and handsome policeman with the handlebar mustache as to where we could hail a taxi. He smiled at my rudimentary attempt at the language and pointed out the direction we should go. "Ou est le taxi, s'il vous plait?" cafe au lait, un sandwich fromage, et "Merci beaucoup!" will be my limited language skills for survival in the event I should again travel abroad.

American female pop culture icons for my generation began with Wilma and Betty, Ginger and Mary Ann, and then graduated to Emma Peel or Agent 99, and Cher or Farrah. Then there was Mary Richards and her best friend, Rhoda Morgenstern. In the eponymous television series, Rhoda returned home from Minneapolis to New York City to open a window dressing and design business. The felt markers and colorful pen sets on her drafting table were evocative of endless career possibilities in the world of art.

When the college admissions counselor from Spokane Falls Community College offered a two-year course in Visual Merchandising and Display Design, the only one of its kind west of the Mississippi, there was no looking back.

The immersive course included training in department store window display, television and theater set design, lighting, mannequin repair, as well as in-store and museum display fabrication. The objective was to capture the attention of the consumer within a few seconds, through the impact of color, contrast, and repetition. Whole semesters were devoted to color and design, brush lettering, drawing composition, and figure drawing. Assignments had to be prepared as if for boardroom presentation. If ink or paint was accidentally dropped onto the hot press board, the project had to be completely redone.

Many of the professors were working artists, and all were masters of their discipline-drawing, painting, sculpting, and jewelry design to name a few. It was an honor to study in the Display Design courses with Gary Ayers, who was the window designer for The Crescent in Spokane, which was famous for the animated corner display at Christmastime. Georg Heimdal's exacting classes in Drawing Composition created some dismay among more than a few students, but staying the course was well worth it. The professor that I learned the most from, and who said the least, was noted artist Dick Ibach—he would simply point out the strengths of the piece we were working on in Figure Drawing.

At historic Fort George Wright, the row of red brick dormitories, originally officers' quarters named after famous battles, became my home away from home, and hours and hours of assignments were completed at the large table in the dining room. I lived in Bourget, named for The Battle of Le Bourget, part of the siege of Paris during the Franco-Prussian War. The college was situated on the bluff next to the fort, offering spectacular views of the Spokane River and it was only a few miles to the Cheney Cowles Museum, now known as the Northwest Museum of Arts and Culture.

A friend's father, Larry Vining, had offered to give the Bug a new coat of Dulux and told me to go to the automotive supply store and pick out a color. It was agonizing trying to make up my mind as to what color the Bug should be. To me, the paint chips were like candy! Should it remain the original stock color of Sea Sand or painted to resemble a ladybug? I settled on Calumet Cream and was over the moon at the results—it looked like an egg! The days that I needed inspiration, the Egg would deliver me to the museum and I would quietly meander through the galleries of longing and wonder how I could get "there."

Chapter 15

Thursday's Child...

Ever curious about our country and the diverse culture in which we live, my desire was to see the United States of America. I just never dreamed that I would dwell in three of the four corners.

In the late 1980s, after seven years of working at a department store in their sign shop, operating a flatbed printing press and a hydraulic print-a-sign, the 1967 Marina Blue, four-door Chevrolet Impala crossed the northern states carrying babies and dreams. The car made its way from Spokane, over the Rocky Mountains, across the Great Plains by Little Bighorn Battlefield, with a side trip to De Smet, South Dakota, to visit the Laura Ingalls Wilder Memorial Society, and safely to our destination of New Jersey.

During that time in the northeast, it pleased me that we were able to take our children, though very young, to visit Valley Forge National Historical Park, Gettysburg Battlefield, Washington Crossing National Park, and the Statue of Liberty. The times that my parents were able to join us on these excursions made it particularly meaningful, as my father had taught World and United States history, with an emphasis on the Civil War.

Where we lived in the city of Trenton there were many elderly people who, with their families, had immigrated as children from Italy, Poland, and Hungary, escaping the catastrophic events of WWI. Behind the crowded rows of red-brick two-family homes, their tiny, immaculate flower and vegetable gardens were filled with tomatoes, peppers, and herbs. On Sundays, the enticing aromas of marinara sauce wafted through the neighborhoods. Was it reminiscent of the old country? Had their childhood recollections of the motherland dissipated? Perhaps the transportive quality of the senses helped grasp the last remnants of a fading memory.

Chapter 16

...Has Far to Go

Seeking a slower pace after six years of crowded, urban frenzy, the 1986 Dark Red Metallic faux-wood paneled, eight-passenger Buick Electra Estate Wagon filled with hope and more kids made its way from the northeast and down the Great Wagon Road to South Carolina.

On a Sunday afternoon in early December, the Ark exited the interstate into the little southern mill village of Enoree. To our surprise there were people, fire engines, utility vehicles, and vintage cars and trucks everywhere. We slowed down and realized that we had just missed being a part of the Enoree Christmas Parade. Our friends said, "Look! They're throwing you a parade!"

With five more miles to go, we stopped at a gas station for milk, traveled through the town of Laurens, and finally drove up to the house we would be renting. I was shocked and astounded. It was a white, two-story, pre-Civil War house built in 1853 according to the date on the chimney. There were French doors on both sides of the fireplace leading out to a side porch. The first thing I noticed were the lavender glass doorknobs. It was a delicate and magical detail that welcomed me to my new home, having always been enchanted by the glass doorknob on the sunny side of Grandma Hyatt's house in Lewiston, turned lavender by years of southern exposure.

Rhapsody in Rose Quartz and Serenity

Appealing as it all was, the task of unpacking, finding my way about the area, and getting the children enrolled in school was overwhelming. Thankfully, everyone was so kind and helpful, and I appreciated that neighborly and mannerly ways still existed in the world.

We believed that we would one day return to Washington State after our tenure in New Jersey, but South Carolina was even farther away. Nearly twenty-five hundred miles separated me from my beloved land of lilacs, locust trees, and wild gypsophila.

Was I destined by my birth on a Thursday to trudge through life on a long and arduous journey in unfamiliar territory? To dwell in the land of unbelief was not productive. Recurring dreams of sparkling lavender, blue, and pink locust trees at Old Kettle Falls and heavenly river valleys appeared in my sleep as if it were glimpses into the eternal, sustained me in my innermost being.

CHAPTER 17

Dreams Take Flight

It had been ten years since I had worked outside the home. My days were filled with raising children, their school and extracurricular activities, grocery shopping, cooking, cleaning, and attempting to keep up with mountains of laundry. My dreams of pursuing a career as an artist had been put on hold in order to gladly devote myself to my family.

However, the innate need to create is a jealous, persistent, and even nagging companion. With four children under the age of ten, there was very little energy to spare. A few unfinished paintings had arrived with me from New Jersey. One day a large, flat crate arrived. Inside the perfectly constructed container that Dad had built was another unfinished work from my college years—a painting of a ballet dancer—with a note from Mom. It said, "Will you please finish this!"

Stephen, Maria, Philip, and John

Regret can be a loathsome character, and I refused to let it take up residence. When the three older children, Philip, Stephen, and Maria were in school, I poured my attention on John, who was two years old. We read, held hands on our walks, and sat on the large carpet of moss near an old apple tree at the corner of the property. In early spring, I could see from the kitchen window the great wall of vines at the edge of the woods gradually turn, to my delight, from gray to lavender. Instead of lilacs and locusts, I was gifted with wisteria, which resembled a marriage of the two. Next to the kitchen on the back corner of the historic house there was a large sunroom with many panes of glass...a studio?

I had no idea where to begin except to finish the paintings I had started. There was a county arts council exhibition advertised in the local paper, so I submitted my work. From that venue, I began receiving requests to teach oil painting. It was a compliment to be asked, and something I could do from home while raising my young family. Patterned after Mr. Pogue's classes from years before, it was a wonderful way to connect with the community, and a local bank generously arranged for us to have an exhibition of the students' work in their town center location.

Over the next few months, I entered some juried exhibitions in surrounding counties and won People's Choice in several of them. What made it even more special was that my mother was present to see the painting that she told me to "please finish" win one of those awards. All that I knew to do was to continue to follow the encouragement and opportunities presented to me. I learned to mix the pigments for humid, teal-green landscapes and of southern skies—French Ultramarine, Alizarin Crimson, Yellow Ochre, and Titanium White, with sunsets glowing peach-colored because of the red clay soil in the atmosphere.

1995 – on my way to my first professional art exhibition

Whenever I was invited to exhibit my work, I did so. The 1995 Light Quasar Blue GMC Safari Van that carried bigger kids, bookbags, sporting equipment, display racks, and paintings was exhausted...but she kept going.

Chapter 18

Southern Folk Hymn

It was a leap of faith to purchase a house in town, but studio and classroom space in the basement made it a sensible decision. The initial tour with the realtor revealed a painter's palette hanging on the wall in the basement. This was an obvious sign, and it did not escape my notice that a lavender glass swan was holding court on the front porch.

Dad was looking forward to driving from Washington State to South Carolina, with a truck full of tools to help with repairs on the house. But it was not to be—he was never able to visit us in that home. In June of 1997 he underwent major gastroesophageal surgery. He had helped my mother recover from a brain aneurysm five years before and she took the best of care for him in the remaining months of his life.

The kids and I waited as many weeks as possible before descending on my folks. It was late July, and they were waiting outside in the shade when we drove up. Dad stood up and walked toward me with his arms outstretched, both of us sobbing as we embraced one another. Understanding the fragility of life and shortness of days, my attempts to make the most of my visit with them felt so feeble. On a late afternoon he said, "Linda, let's go for a drive." He was still recovering from the traumatic surgery, so I drove, avoiding as many bumps in the road as possible. Neither of us spoke, but after a few miles he remarked, "You're a good driver." It was one of the greatest compliments that he ever gave me.

His keen observation of people and situations could be distilled into five words or less. He said what he meant and meant what he said. Bullying did not fly at school or in the classroom, and he cared deeply that all of his students had a pleasant life at home.

In November he knew his health was not going to improve so, before the snows flew, he went to the cemetery to measure and make sure that his own final resting place was properly and accurately marked near the dogwood whose leaves were dark red from autumn frosts. By January, the surgeon recommended that I travel home to be with him in his final days. Dad once said that he did not want anyone to hover around his deathbed. Sensitive to his request, I sat in a chair away from the bed, and for the first time, I understood that heaven is not up in the sky, but was in the room, surrounding us with grace.

The gravesite of Thomas Hyatt, his date of death, Feb. 3, 1843, located at Bethlehem Methodist Church in Union, South Carolina

At my father's funeral, blue spruce trees stood watch in a foot of snow, and a cloud of witnesses enveloped us as the bagpiper played from the little hill in the cemetery. In my hurry I had not thought to pack a somber black coat suitable for a funeral—so a bright red coat with fur trim paid respect in its own way.

"What Wondrous Love Is This" was selected for the service, but I did not realize at the time that it is a Southern folk hymn. I would not know for another ten years that the land on which the gas station stood, where we stopped for milk upon our arrival outside of Laurens was originally on, or very near, a ten-thousand-acre Revolutionary War land grant awarded to my father's Duvall ancestor. The astonishment would have been immeasurable for him to visit his third great grandfather Thomas Hyatt's resting place thirty miles from where I landed in South Carolina.

CHAPTER 19

The Guardians

The void was immense...my North Star that should have been keenly observed, the compass that could have been carried more often, the map by which directions should have been followed more closely, and the textbook that could be wisely referred to was gone. When my mother asked me to design their memorial stone, I wished that I had studied perspective drawing in my father's classes. She had ordered Gray Cloud granite so, at my dining room table, her idea of a Cessna 172 with blue stripes and its registration number flying through the clouds was translated. Violets were her favorite, so I referred to a design that her mother had embroidered depicting a small bouquet for the lower right corner.

Working at the dining room table was at first a necessity to be able to stop and prepare meals, to make sure the kids' homework was done, or to do laundry. A company of at least five or more middle-school-age boys would traipse though and then be instructed to leave their weapons at the door. Following my orders, they would turn around and do so and then continue on their march through the house. I peered out the front door and saw the arsenal of walking sticks, BB guns, slingshots, jack-knives, canteens, etc. on the front porch and shook my head and hoped it was for the purpose of developing survival skills.

Sometimes angels drop out of the sky in the form of a brash WWII paratrooper from Massachusetts. Walter Catarius went through Marine Corps boot camp at Parris Island when tents served as barracks. He would swim beside the ship in the South Pacific to pass the time and witnessed the raising of the United States flag on Mount Suribachi. Assigned as his assistant at a summer arts program for children, he later told me that he noticed the exhaustion and maybe even frustration on my countenance as I pulled up in the station wagon full of my troops—and that I was wearing red. In a booming voice he would exclaim, "I didn't raise my kids! I survived them!" He never spared anyone the cold hard truth, but understood completely and was always in my corner.

Angels arrive as an expert on colonial roads, a solver of mysteries, and as a trumpet player of jazz standards. Mr. David George called me one day and said, "Linda, are you sitting down?! You are related to half of the upstate!" As someone that sometimes felt like an outsider, it was music to my ears—he was able to connect me to my Southern roots.

Then there is the archangel who served two tours in the Vietnam War, with missions that required crawling through the jungles of Southeast Asia to disable downed aircraft, and he was awarded the service-wide honor of Man of the Year in 1968 with Chuck Yeager as his commanding officer. Retired CMSgt Donald Kisamore, USAF, was speaking for a multitude when he told of returning to American soil and being spit upon by the ones whose right to do so was being protected by the ones they reviled and vilified. For a split second the pain would overtake the guarded memory. My mother's brother, my uncle Don, has always been there for my family.

To describe in a few paragraphs the service of these individuals to their country, community, and their families and friends, is utterly insufficient and totally inadequate. What I do know is that I've been supremely fortunate, thankful, and blessed to have the care of people of this level of integrity and quality in my life.

CHAPTER 20

The Gift

One of my paintings of an Irish lad in a rain slicker, leaning on a walking stick on Croagh Patrick, was getting more than a few requests for reproduction prints. I was graciously given permission from National Geographic photographer, Fr Don Doll SJ of Creighton University, to reproduce my painting of his original, iconic photograph. Hall Printing in High Point, North Carolina, was highly recommended for fine art lithographic printing, so the painting was delivered to their place of operation for print preparation and setup. It was a whole new and daunting experience as the experts explained the process and generously showed me the work of noted artists who trusted the company with reproducing hundreds of thousands of dollars worth of artwork—Mort Künstler and Bob Timberlake, to name a few.

The Gift

The Vice President of Sales, Mr. Cliff Snider, who was particularly kind and encouraging, liked my work very much and said it was reminiscent of one of his favorite artists and illustrators, N.C. Wyeth. For me, those were magic words. Mr. Snider's white beard and gentle personality hinted at a fulfillment of another calling in his life—Santa Claus! I am not sure how the dialogue started, but there was a phone call to me at my home in Laurens, South Carolina, from Santa Claus himself, asking if I would be interested in painting his portrait.

It was not my practice to turn down work, but honestly, my relationship with the celebration of the Christmas holiday season opened up a big box of mixed feelings for me, but an invitation to portray in oils one of the most recognizable and beloved figures in the world became one of the greatest gifts I was ever blessed with. Santa Claus had found me in the Carolinas...

Santa Cliff provided me with a photograph taken by his friend, a professional photographer, and added to the image were accoutrements of what Santa might be employing in his workshop. The props interjected into the scene are carving tools and a wooden nativity set as Santa admires his handiwork of a little lamb, while lights from a decorated Christmas tree reflect off the tabletop.

The Gift lithograph debuted at the Holiday Market with The Remarque Gallery at the Greensboro Coliseum and to our surprise, exceeded our expectations with an immediate and favorable response, and seemed to take on a life of its own. Santa Cliff's friend penned the poetry that introduced the scripture: "If you look closely, you will see him smiling at his own symbolism, as he reverently holds the true gift in his hands…'Look, the Lamb of God who takes away the sin of the world!'" (John 1:29, NIV).

Chapter 21

The Lamb

With the success of the first signed and numbered limited edition print, Santa Cliff and I decided to collaborate on a second painting for a new lithograph. Santa's seamstress, retired home economics teacher Mrs. Eva Rae Clark, created the most elegant and beautiful cloak, worthy of any cinematic or theater production. Flying reindeer were embossed as detail into the evergreen-colored velvet lined with red satin, and the magnificent garment was trimmed with fur repurposed from a vintage raccoon coat.

The Lamb

I recalled seeing an image from a publication depicting a shepherd in Germany, in a green duster work coat, leading a flock of sheep and carrying a lamb. For the painting I envisioned the Santa Claus figure emerging from a cathedral-like forest, gently carrying a rescued lamb. There were moments when I felt hesitant and wondered if I was traveling down the right path, not fully understanding what I was trying to convey with this image. The tree limbs in the foreground that form a cross were perhaps a result of my subconscious and had to be pointed out to me. What kept coming to mind about the composition, is that as one goes through the trials and tribulations of life, with faith, hope, and love, we can emerge with the Lamb. Mrs. Janie Snider, Santa's wife, selected the perfect Bible verse from Ezekiel 34:12 (NIV) which created a cohesive completion for the concept: "As a shepherd looks after his scattered flock when he is with them, so I will look after my sheep."

Little did we know that the new lithograph depicting the return from a search for the lost would be presented less than two months after the unimaginable and horrific events of September 11, 2001.

CHAPTER 22

The Light

The Light

On one of Santa Cliff Snider's visits to Laurens for an appearance, a photo opportunity would be planned for the next lithograph concept. I envisioned Santa in his beautiful evergreen-colored velvet coat in the sanctuary of the historic Church of the Epiphany, carrying a candle, and reverently approaching the altar. The December twilight created a warm and inviting scene inside the church that was established in 1846.

The elements of the church pew, the figure, and the gothic window created a pleasing repetition of shapes that suggest the numeration of the Holy Trinity. The halo around the candlelight occurred naturally in the amazing reference photo taken by professional photographer, Suellen Holmes, and she explained how the atmospheric conditions in the church contributed to this. Again, Janie Snider selected the perfect scripture verse to grace the image: "…let your light shine before others, that they may see your good deeds and glorify your Father in heaven." (Matt. 5:16, NIV).

CHAPTER 23

The Journey

The Journey

On one of Santa's pilgrimages to Laurens County, we were kindly allowed access to some pastureland along the Enoree River. The afternoon sun cast a pleasing, early-winter ambiance as I photographed Santa Cliff in his green robe with his walking stick, journeying along the gently flowing river. I imagined him as a shepherd leading his flock beside the water and juxtaposed sheep into the image—seven, being Santa Cliff's favorite number, and painted the trees on opposite sides of the river to connect and reach out to one another.

The verse so perfectly selected was, "He has shown you, O mortal, what is good. And what does the Lord require of you? To act justly and to love mercy and to walk humbly with your God" (Mic. 6:8, NIV).

Chapter 24

The Message

As a child, I would imagine Santa in his sleigh and the harnessed reindeer flying through dark blue velvet skies, as he scanned the little town below for a good place to land.

Not sure even where to begin on this fifth Santa painting, my request to Santa Cliff was a reference photo of him in his sleigh posing as if he were driving his team. I had always admired N.C. Wyeth's painting of *The Ore Wagon*, but this was taking on a different approach than what was first envisioned. I needed a vantage point that was high in the sky and the only one viable was a photo taken on an August afternoon from Tiger Highway as one travels down into the Colville Valley.

The Message

Next was the night sky. For many years as a "bleacher mom," I would absorb the atmosphere between innings at many ball games and observe the sky as the sun went down and the lights came on and imagine what colors I could mix to get the perfect tones of twilight.

The landscape in the painting began to include the lights of Kettle Falls, Our Lady of the Valley Convent, Colville, the Cross on Colville Mountain, and the local airport where my father had flown in and out of in his Cessna 172. Depicted under one of the runners of the sleigh is the light of my parents' home on Monumental Mountain. In the bag of gifts to be delivered are items that represent my own children—toys that were special to them and talents they have.

I wanted to incorporate a message in the stars and again, Janie Snider came up with the perfect message of "Peace on Earth," and my dear friend Mr. David George suggested that musical notes float out of the toy trumpet. I was grateful for these ideas—the notes became the music of the stars in a dark blue velvet night proclaiming a hope for all people. "May the God of Peace...that great Shepherd of the sheep, equip you with everything good for doing his will…" (Heb. 13:20-21, NIV).

Chapter 25

The Hour

Santa's wardrobe designer and seamstress, Mrs. Eva Rae Clark, brought her artistry and expertise to a whole new level of Christmas wonder and warmth. From his attic, Santa Cliff had recovered a crazy quilt pieced by his grandmother and great-grandmother with the hope that Mrs. Eva Rae could work her magic creating a "Coat of Many Colors," reminiscent of his favorite Bible story. She was hesitant to cut into the treasure, but Santa Cliff convinced her that it was not doing any good being hidden away in storage when it could begin a conversation about God's love and faithfulness.

The Hour

How could anyone not be inspired by this fabulous raiment? I imagined Santa with a princely pose in a bishop's chair holding a scepter. Suellen Holmes was again commissioned to photograph Santa Cliff in the historic Church of the Epiphany with the olive wood bas relief of *The Last Supper*, carved in San Antonio, Ecuador, in the background behind the altar. In his hand, Santa is holding a pocket watch, checking to see if it's time to depart for his Christmas Eve flight. The scripture chosen was from Luke 12:40 (NIV): "You also must be ready, because the Son of Man will come at an hour when you do not expect Him."

For me, it was the most technically difficult of all the seven images. The photo reference was taken at midday, and I wanted the rays of light to appear as late afternoon or early evening, and had to imagine and adjust how that hour of daylight would affect the elements of figure, fabric, metals, and wood. With the deadline looming to finish the painting in time for printing for the Holiday Market in November, it didn't help that it was the weekend of "Squealin' on the Square," a local October celebration featuring a Kansas City BBQ Society sanctioned cook-off and vintage car show. The day was very warm, so the windows were open, and the wonderful aromas of a great southern tradition drifted through the house and taunted me even though I lived a mile from the festivities on the town square—a delicious-smelling, but non-participatory distraction!

Even though I considered *The Hour* the most difficult to paint, it is also my personal favorite, maybe because it turned out better than I thought possible. I also love the challenge of painting the appearance of textures in fabric, harkening back to the photos of awe-inspiring paintings of historic figures by Hans Holbein the Younger and Jan van Eyck in my father's textbooks.

Chapter 26

The Spirit

For several years the idea of Santa Claus releasing a white dove into a winter forest was a recurring thought and I mentioned the concept to Santa Cliff. The image in my mind rested for a year or two until one day, Santa Cliff called me with some very exciting news—that Sunday at church, the pastor told the congregation that a white dove was perched on the portico as parishioners entered the sanctuary—a sign and message from above!

The Spirit

My mother enjoyed her role as my western agent and took great delight in delivering the latest Christmas lithograph to her friends who collected the Santa series. When I told her of my idea and this newest development, she was so excited and exclaimed, "The song 'On the Wings of a Snow White Dove' keeps coming to me!"... another confirmation that we were heading in the right direction.

In an effort to find a snowy forest scene, Santa Cliff and Janie had to drive west toward the Blue Ridge Mountains for the perfect reference photo, while I began reading about doves and metaphorical meanings associated with them.

As I had also been researching my southern roots for five years previous, I never would have imagined that every trip taken to High Point and Greensboro brought us only twenty miles from one of my ancestral homes in Randolph County, North Carolina. The historic McMasters Cemetery is where my sixth great-grandfather, Cpt. Duncan Neil McCollum, rests with his wife, Ester, and other family members. As I continued my search about where my people came from and the origin of the surname and its variations, I learned that it honors Colmcille or Columba, a 6th century Irish monk, missionary, and evangelist who founded Scotland's Iona Abbey—and it gave me chills to discover that in Latin the name Columba means "dove."

We debuted *The Spirit* at the 2013 Holiday Market, again in Greensboro, North Carolina, to the ever-wonderful experience of greeting returning collectors and meeting new ones, who never failed to express interest in what inspired each of the seven images—the last which reads, "But the fruit of the Spirit is love, joy, peace, forbearance, kindness, goodness, faithfulness, gentleness, and self-control" (Gal. 5:22, NIV).

Chapter 27

Dark and Stormy November

Two thousand and thirteen was a very strange and busy year. The autumn before, my youngest child, John, flew the nest and reported for boot camp at Parris Island, having enlisted in the United States Marine Corps, as did his older brother Stephen a few years before. The eldest, Philip, had enlisted in the U.S. Army even before that. When the Marine Corps recruiter called for my daughter Maria, he had to laugh when my reply to him was, "Unless pink stilettos are standard issue, she will probably not sign."

For months I had been working on the new Santa painting to debut in November, preparing for a juried show and a one-person exhibition, *Collateral Twilight,* also set for November at Carolina Gallery in Spartanburg, South Carolina.

Dark and Stormy November

Ladybugs...ladybugs everywhere in glossy advertisements, perfume bottles, red Volkswagen Beetles, and in the media, and after nearly twenty years, I was feeling a disconnect with my time in the South and could not understand why. It was a little unnerving as I remembered the ladybug straight pins my mother gifted me with fifty years before. I thought about how Melissa and I had been apart for nearly that length of time. Sometimes I would imagine what it would be like to have my sister and closest friend at this age. What would she look like, and would she have been taller than I? What career would she have chosen? I kept getting older and further away from my beloved four-year-old Melissa. One day, in what seemed like a comforting thought, vision, or visitation, I sensed that she was ageless, in her glorified body, and had been my guardian angel all these years, and the appearance of ladybugs was a playful sign and symbol of her presence.

In October, a friend of my mother's called and insisted that I needed to make the trip to Washington State and assess my mother's increasingly frail health. I would speak to Mom several times a week and she never let on about any dire health problems because that would have opened up the possibility of losing her independence. So, between scheduled career appearances, I traveled to Washington for a week's stay and understood why her friends were concerned. In great pain, she would cry out at night to God, Jesus, and her mother, but still fought against scheduling an appointment with her doctor.

I drove her to Spokane where the physician explained that she had only half of normal heart function—if she were to fall and break a limb, they would be unable to operate. I brought in enough firewood to place on the deck for easy access for her for the week that I would be back in South Carolina. Once there, I packed a box of clothes and a box of art supplies and shipped them to myself at my mother's address for an undetermined length of time.

Dreading her resistance of the next steps in care, her brother, my uncle Don, and his wife, my aunt Sherry, met me at the airport a few days before Thanksgiving. They told me that she was already in the hospital, having fallen off the kitchen chair, with a cracked rib yet undetected. An ambulance was called and this woman—all of four feet eleven inches tall and a hundred pounds—refused to allow the emergency personnel to carry her out on the stretcher according to procedure, so she walked out, steadied by her neighbor.

My only solace was that she was getting the care she desperately needed. It was a "dark and stormy November" and thus became the title of a painting I began working on. My stay was indefinite as her condition was precarious, and I wanted to be there for her as she had been for me all of my life.

As I was searching for paperwork my mother needed, I came across my father's wallet that she had lovingly put away. In it were all of his important licenses, including Washington Air Search and Rescue of which he was very proud. There was also a photo of Melissa, and one of his older brother James Jerome Hyatt who had passed away, and a note written in his handsome, steady handwriting—from Ecclesiastes 3:1-8 (KJV), "To every thing there is a season..."

CHAPTER 28

The Sun Rises in the East

Mom was never able to live in her home again by the order of her doctor, and the next ten months of her life were spent in hospital and nursing facilities. I tried to make sure that she was as comfortable as possible in her new surroundings, ever thankful for good friends who visited, called, and sent well wishes to us both. I missed only one day to visit her due to snowy winter roads. The roles had reversed, and I was forced to match wits with her strong personality. One day she said, "Well! Aren't you the bossy one!" and my reply was, "Well! I learned from the BEST!" and that made it okay.

On July 4th, 2014, with a panoramic view of the Colville Valley, while watching fireworks from her room, we were unaware that Logan—her first great grandchild and my first grandchild—was just born on the east coast. It was such a happy and glorious day for our family. I thank heaven that she was able to know this absolutely wonderful news.

On the morning of August 5th, the nurse at the hospital called to tell me that my mother had passed, and even though it was not unexpected, the finality and loss always is. I drove east across the valley as the sun was rising over Dominion Mountain and the song on the radio that met the morning was "American Pie." As I entered the hospital, I was barely able to meet the eyes of the kind and sympathetic receptionists.

The sun shone softly into the room as I slowly made my way to her bedside and placed my hand on her hand. I sat down and laid my head next to her. I had never seen her so still, even in her sleep. As warm tears streamed down my face, the chaplain, with his kind and gentle demeanor, asked if he could step into the room. I don't know how these very special human beings do this on a regular basis. He spoke metaphorically from the passage Matthew 24:27 (KJ21), "For as the lightning cometh out of the east and shineth even unto the west, so shall also the coming of the Son of man be."

The woman who survived the unimaginable loss of a child, a meticulous bookkeeper and baker of pies, a formidable softball player and fierce opponent, the woman who worked so hard physically and mentally with purpose and good intent, who suffered a brain aneurysm in her late fifties, and the woman who said that every night she dreamed of fighting battles in the Coliseum—Germania Superior DNA in its most concentrated form—was at peace.

Mountain Ash limbs ripe with orange berries from trees that she had planted so long ago for the wild birds' sake, and cedar boughs gathered from her land were delivered to the florist for the large arrangement for the casket, to which white and cobalt-colored flowers were added.

My mother in Texas – about 1954

Loved ones who attended the funeral stood in the shade of the dogwood tree that she planted and kept alive so many years before, and a large, brown butterfly fluttered over as the eulogy was being read. A dear friend, musician Justin Johnson, sang and played some of her favorite tunes on his guitar at the gravesite such as "On the Wings of a Dove," "Onward, Christian Soldiers," "Take Me Home, Country Roads," and her most favorite song of all, "Friends in Low Places," ushered us home.

Wife...Mother...Grandma...Phyllis...Greek for "green bough..."

Chapter 29

Follow the Yellow Brick Road

The tornado that had me in its grip for months and even years unceremoniously spewed me out. There was no technicolor dreamscape, munchkins, ruby slippers, or good witches to wave their magic wand and show me where to start my journey.

I was thrown into the realities of pressure tanks, waterlines, well pumps, cleaning stove pipes and pellet stoves, chopping wood, and trying to find the septic tank when the grass was not greener that time of year. There were so many decisions, sorting, packing, storing, and more decisions while I continued to paint and ship work back to South Carolina. It had taken twenty years to establish my career in the southeast and I was unsure what the future might hold.

Drifter

A fellow artist had shared on social media about opportunities for artists with the National Park Service, to be selected to complete a work of art for the NPS permanent collection of a designated park. I sent an email to Dear Sir/Madam at the Lake Roosevelt National Recreation Area's Kettle Falls ranger station, inquiring about their Artist-in-Residence Program and expressing my interest in applying. Park Ranger Brandon Andrews had arrived from Chiricahua National Monument in Arizona three weeks before and was immediately put on forest fire duty. It must have literally felt like jumping from the frying pan into the fire.

Upon his return, he answered my email and requested to view images of my work, after which he was able to visit my home studio. My hope was that I would be able to serve in this capacity for the region I had deeply missed and dreamed about. Brandon said that if I so chose, the residency was mine.

At Chiricahua, he had instituted a program that received about eighty applicants from all over the world. I asked him how many artists applied for this particular one and he said, "Just you, but I didn't need to look any further." The requirement was that I create one artwork for the permanent collection for the headquarters at Coulee Dam, Washington. But how can you paint just one when there are one-hundred and thirty miles of vista from Grand Coulee Dam to the United States/Canada border?

Hoping for an invitation to hold an exhibition, I called the Northwest Museum of Arts and Culture in Spokane and spoke with the curator, John, explaining my endeavor with the Lake Roosevelt National Recreation Area, and that 2016 also happened to be the centennial celebration of the formation of the National Park Service. He said that the exhibition board would be meeting next week and would not meet again for six months, and to send some images of my work. A few days later, John called and asked me, "Would you prefer June, July, or September?" I was supremely grateful, and my request was for September 2016 as it would give me more time. He asked how many paintings I could deliver, and my answer was, "I think I can finish thirty."

Over the next ten months of my tenure at Lake Roosevelt, I painted as though I would never have the opportunity again. Thirty paintings were completed in the time it took to paint ten, and I proudly delivered the collection *The Rising* by the end of August in a U-Haul to the Museum of Arts and Culture.

My decision to name the collection *The Rising* was in reference to the building of Grand Coulee Dam and the flooding that ensued, introducing a new era of hydroelectric power, irrigation, and agricultural opportunities to the arid Columbia River Basin. Tragically, the hunting, fishing, and burial grounds of Native Americans were desecrated, and their thousands-years-old way of life will never be the same.

The collection's title held special meaning to me personally. Throughout the years, there were many wonderful friends and mentors who supported and encouraged me. Yet at times, psychological and spiritual battles I encountered left me feeling as though I was alone, adrift in an ocean with no life preserver. As soon as I could catch a breath, the next huge wave would bear down on me. I did not know how much more I could endure before I would be crushed under the weight of simply being human and embracing my gift, which had always been vital to my self-preservation and salvation. I was forced to find the strength within myself to learn to rise above any ugliness or negativity that came my way.

Chapter 30

Make-Up Artist

Park Ranger Brandon was promoted to Park Chief at San Juan National Historic Park, and I was extremely honored to again be invited by him to be an Artist-in-Residence for this magical island with a fascinating history, surrounded by the Salish Sea. Nineteen paintings were delivered for an exhibition titled *Do They Miss Me at Home?*, on behalf of the Park Service to the San Juan Islands Museum of Art at Friday Harbor, Washington. My fears of career stagnancy were no longer, as over a ten-year period, two museum exhibitions, two one-person, and ten group shows kept me extremely and happily busy, with even more scheduled.

Do They Miss Me at Home?

Between the deadlines, and even during, are the quiet moments to reflect; hoping that my adult children and my grandchildren are safe, happy, and thriving in their life; hoping that all the love and support I was given by family and friends was reciprocated.

While connecting the dots in my life and artistic journey, patterns began to emerge, both good and unhealthy, such as over-compensating, people-pleasing, and times when I allowed myself to be bullied and manipulated. How did I arrive at that? To think everyone had, reasonably, the same values as my parents was extremely naive. Even though I refused to be a victim or make excuses, it still created obstacles that needed to be addressed and overcome for a content and fulfilling life. I allowed myself a few years for some personal, psychological, and spiritual archeology.

I began to give my five-year-old self a break and started looking at my life as a nonjudgmental observer. Responses to grief are highly personal and specific to each individual; I can only speak about my own experience. At age seven, heaven now possessed my angel sister, and I had to live as though I would be good enough to see her again. She was so precious and sweet, I must have been the "bad" one. Was the eight-inch scar on her back where angel wings had been?

Moments of sadness on my parents' faces must be my fault for some unexplained reason.

Almost entirely self-imposed, my teen years and young adulthood were spent hyper focused; avoiding bad behavior, peer pressure, and protecting myself from any harm so that my parents would not have to suffer more disappointment, trauma, or loss of another child. In my subconscious, the plague of anxiety and fear had attached itself and haunted me, remedied by staying busy and trying to cover it all up with a smile.

As a painting is never finished, love for my children and grandchildren, my parents' love, support, and wisdom, my life's work, and my faith continues to be my saving grace.

Dan Bennett of Eye on Brevard in North Carolina captured this photo of a baby robin peering through an art gallery window at one of my nest paintings

CHAPTER 31

Plant One Acorn

The Melissa Oak

My surroundings could not be more of a comfort. The master craftsmanship of my father's woodworking, the bricks for the fireplace salvaged from his first school in Kettle Falls, and also mine, warm our home, and trees my mother propagated shade the yard; pink plum, varieties of apple and cherry, mountain ash, buckeye, black walnut, Norway maples, and the most special of all: what we call the Melissa Oak. My sister once said, "Plant one acorn, get one squirrel," so at this homeplace, an oak tree profoundly flourishes.

An invitation to serve on the board at the Meyers Falls Cemetery Association was willingly and dutifully accepted. On a workday there, in preparation for Memorial Day, a blue feather danced across the grass in front of me, so I put it on the nearest gravesite, which happened to be the original town's founder's. I continued raking and the feather blew again in front of me as a gentle reminder of Melissa's wish for a bluebird to sit on her headstone, so I picked it up again and walked over to place it with her under the pink dogwood.

As a heartwarming surprise, a friend arranged for me to ride in my dad's 1935 Ford three window coupe, now completely restored, before it left for its new home on the coast. Now, a 2008 Graystone Metallic four-wheel drive Trailblazer—a presidential detail fleet vehicle—delivers loads of paintings to the wonderful galleries that represent my work.

When *It's a Mad, Mad, Mad, Mad World* airs, I remember the fun we had when Dad took me to the theater to see the film on the big screen, delighting in all the vintage cars and airplanes, and how we laughed and laughed at the silliness of human nature. I still think that *Gilligan's Island* is brilliantly written with infectious humor, resourcefulness, and good attitude.

When the Byrds' version of "Turn! Turn! Turn!" and Don McLean's "American Pie" play on the radio, I let the moments seep into my heart as a sweet visitation.

All the grandsons, Logan, Mason, Theo, Milo, and Michael, have special dates associated with their own: Independence Day, Dominican Republic Independence Day, Flag Day, the publishing of "The Star-Spangled Banner" in 1814, and Grandpa Byron Kisamore's birthday, respectively. Meadow Milly-Rose, a girl with green eyes and hints of red in her hair, was born on July 21, 2023, on what would have been John Hyatt's eighty-ninth birthday. Last, but certainly not least, Ruth Delores was born on February 25, 2025, on what would have been Grandma Pansy Kisamore's one hundred and fifteenth birthday.

V is for Violet

When not watching great cinematographic films and retro television series, I enjoy watching cooking shows such as the Barefoot Contessa and chef Nick Stellino's programs on PBS. Nick's finely tailored suits, his eyebrows with a personality of their own, his exuberant storytelling of memories evoked by his family's cuisine in his beloved Italy, his great love and adoration for his wife and how the success of a new recipe is measured by her smile, made for a lovely vision of domestic and artistic bliss. Where was my very own Nick Stellino?

While I did not get to New York like Rhoda, my elliptical journey took me to places I would have never dreamt of, where I would find Santa Claus and "meet" the ancestors I may never have known about. The English nursery rhyme, "Monday's Child," has taken on a new, more hopeful and adventurous meaning for me than how I interpreted it when I was young.

A few years ago, a journalist extended an invitation for my work to be featured in his online lifestyle magazine, The New York Optimist. John Sebastian is an artist, writer, actor, and musician, and now, when we are not painting, writing, and creating, his strong hands peel garlic for the most delicious sauce, as he speaks lovingly of growing up on Long Island in a large Italian family of musicians, luthiers, and creatives, and wonderful memories of family gatherings with great food and music. New York came to me.

I still pick up metal washers when I find them, representing my own personal Odyssey, and maintain an active awareness for the signs and wonders I will be blessed with every day.

As if preparing a feast for guests to enjoy, I still feel most comfortable and productive working at the dining room table. My more recent landscape paintings, in my mind and soul, appear dreamlike...suspended between heaven and earth...so that I am not too far from the loved ones who have gone before. Between waking and sleep, I've seen my angel.

Never The End

Linda Bird

by Don Kisamore

In the spring of 2000, a small wren decided to build a nest inside a wreath that I had hung on the wall adjacent to my kitchen entrance door. The wreath had hung there several years. It was a handmade gift sent to me from my niece, Linda Hyatt Cancél, an established artist and Washington native residing in Laurens, SC. I thought at the time that it was a dumb thing to do to place the wreath within inches of a busy access door.

I had just returned from my first visit with my new-born grandson in western Washington. Apparently, the little wren had decided that since nobody was around during my absence, she would take over the sheltered place for her nest. As time went on, the daily encounters with me discouraged her, and she abandoned her abode and went elsewhere. About a week later, Linda showed up. My first glimpse of her was memorable. She sat on the porch railing and checked me out through the kitchen window, turning her head from side to side, flicking her tail and puffing up her topknot. She was pale green and gray, with light-streaked feathers on her wings and back. She continued to stare boldly at me, and I noticed a definite ring around her eyes. She stayed put for a while, then flew away towards the Mountain Ash tree. I didn't think much about it until several days later when I noticed some activity around the wren's partially built nest. Linda had decided that even though the nest was second-hand, the advantages of a covered porch and security from predators outweighed the nuisance of being disturbed by people coming and going. Thus, a decade-long love affair was being put in motion by a little green bird called Linda.

As time went on, we determined that Linda and her mate, Larry, were known as Western Flycatchers. There is almost no difference between the male and female's plumage in markings and coloration. In fact, the only way that we can tell them apart is by their demeanor. Linda is a little saucier and Larry seems confused at times. Can we relate? Every year you can almost mark their return date on the calendar, and we start looking for them about the tenth of June. I do not know the lifespan of this particular species, but I find it hard to believe that this is the same pair of birds. They have brought us some fond memories, what with the perils and pitfalls Mother Nature provides. On one occasion, a large raven planned to rob Linda's nest of her hatch. We warded him off and my wife, Sherry, bought a life-sized plastic owl and placed it on the porch rail near the nest. That seemed to do the trick. When Linda makes her annual Spring debut, she greets us by sitting on the porch rail by the dinner triangle, making sure that we see her. When she has ascertained that no one has invaded her territory, she then spruces up the original nest, adding material and arranging it just so. Then we see very little of her for a week or so.

Almost by magic, the first egg appears, grayish-mottled-speckled. As days go by, several more are added; up to as many as five. When Linda is satisfied with her endeavors and decides to sit on the eggs, our lifestyle changes. We lock the kitchen door from the inside and post a large "LINDA" sign near the door handle. We must then use another entrance for our coming and goings. Initially, we had just two entrances to the house. Subsequently we built an addition which provided another entryway, so that we don't have to walk all the way around the house to avoid upsetting Linda at her labors. It's our "Linda" door.

On one occasion I noticed that three of her newly laid eggs had been ejected from the nest and were lying unbroken on the porch mat. I carefully picked them up and placed them back into the nest. Linda hatched all three successfully. Yay! The babies grow very quickly. In a matter of days, they evolve from tiny pink skin and yellow beaks to beady-eyed little rascals, eyeing the world suspiciously. We name all of them, using names starting with the letter "L." Linda's mate, Larry, is sometimes confused. I say that because at times he flies to the wrong nest. You see, when we built the addition on the house, we added a wreath to that entrance door as well, albeit one made of plastic. Larry, in his role of provider while Linda is sitting on the nest, appears with a beakful of insects, and sometimes approaches the wrong wreath and flits around awhile before he figures it out.

Linda's presence has been spiritual for us. On at least two occasions, she and Larry have shown up well after their brood has departed the nest as if to thank us for our indulgence and bid us farewell until next year. They get so close I can almost reach out and touch them, and they "talk" to me. I will not see them until the next year. Years ago, Linda Hyatt Cancél visited us and learned the saga of Linda Bird. From that introduction, the legend was born. Linda and her nest found her way into paintings. I am now eighty-eight years of age, and Linda Bird and her descendants have been a part of my life for over two decades. I cherish her spirit and honor her accomplishments. She is the hardest working bird I have ever known.

Thoughts from Santa Cliff

The Gift

When I had "a real job," I had the opportunity to work with many talented artists. As a salesman for a fine art company, I was able to help artists in the reproduction of their original paintings into limited-edition fine art prints. I met Linda Cancél in 2000 and I was easily impressed by her realistic oil portraits. Maybe she was intrigued by the fact that I had a unique resemblance to Santa Claus, because she asked me if I would allow her to paint my portrait. Little did I know at the time that her innocent request would be the catalyst for transformation in my career. I shared a favorite photo taken of me by one of the first photographers to photograph me as Santa Claus, Brian Hayes. Brian had unexpectedly passed away, so his photo held a special place in my heart that always reminded me of his sweet spirit. In the photograph, I was holding a miniature carving of an elf. My wife, Janie, made the comment, "I think you should be holding a carving from a Nativity set to remind people of why we celebrate Christmas." Linda, a fellow believer, was delighted with Janie's suggestion, so she painted Santa holding a carved lamb from a Nativity set.

I was so flattered and delighted with the original oil painting Linda created of *The Gift* that I purchased it and it hangs in the dining room of our home. It represents the beginnings of a series of paintings by various artists that now numbers more than seventy images. But *The Gift* always reminds me of the reason we celebrate Christmas and the reason I feel portraying Santa Claus is my Christian calling. But perhaps more important than that is the fact that I have developed a deep and abiding friendship with Linda, that continues to inspire ideas for paintings together.

Once the original painting was finished, we had many discussions about what to title the reproductions we planned to make of it. I showed it to another artist friend, who is also an evangelist. Knowing me and my desire to serve God through my Santa ministry, he penned the following words: "If you look closely, you will see him smiling at his own symbolism, as he reverently holds the true gift in his hands…'Look, the

Lamb of God who takes away the sin of the world!'" (John 1:29, NIV). With those words we knew the title of Linda's first Santa painting was to be *The Gift*.

As an interesting side story to painting, when I was in elementary school, I took violin lessons in a little one-room schoolhouse at Ray Street School in High Point, NC. The schoolhouse was called "The Little Red School House." Unfortunately, Ray Street School was destroyed in a fire in the late 1950s and the Little Red School House fell into disrepair. A couple of years ago, a fund drive was started to move the schoolhouse to the grounds of the High Point Museum near my home and restore it to its original condition. I wanted to help in raising funds for restoration, and since I annually appear at the holiday open house at the museum, I decided to donate a number of reproductions of *The Gift* to the museum to help with the moving and restoration. *The Gift* continues giving because at the Christmas open house at the High Point Museum, Santa will receive guests in The Little Red School House where he first learned to play the violin when he was in the fourth grade.

The Lamb

I was meeting with my fellow employees in the conference room of Riverwood Hall in Lexington, NC on September 11, 2001, when one of our owners called and told us to turn on the television. We watched in disbelief as we witnessed the twin towers of the World Trade Center in New York City collapse and change life in America forever.

In my portrayal of Santa Claus, I have always tried to create costumes and accessories that make my appearance unique from other Christmas characters. I am blessed to have a friend who is a retired home economics teacher that I collaborate with in creating the garments that I wear. She is part of my creative tribe and no matter how challenging my ideas are, she always enthusiastically accepts whatever idea I present to her...at 83 years young! During one of my frequent visits to thrift shops and antique stores, I found a full-length vintage men's raccoon fur coat. After paying only one hundred dollars for the coat, I decided the fur would make the perfect trim for a "Father Christmas" robe for Santa in green velvet and not the traditional red. On my next trip visiting Linda at her home in Laurens, SC I took my new robe to see how she liked it. She was so impressed with the new look that she wanted to feature it in her next Santa painting.

You can imagine how surprised I was when I first saw *The Lamb* depicting Santa carrying a lost lamb out of the forest. How could a painting symbolize the tragedy we had just experienced and still offer hope for all? Even the fallen trees in the foreground forming a cross remind us of "The Lamb of God" who was slain, and that there was still hope for our wounded nation. Appropriately in the time of need that America faced in

2001, the scripture featured read: "As a shepherd looks after his scattered flock when he is with them, so I will look after my sheep" (Ezek. 34:12, NIV).

The Light

On my next trip to Laurens to see Linda in 2003, she took me and a professional photographer to a beautiful pre-Civil War church in the quaint southern town. We were the only ones there, and a sense of awe and reverence and an appreciation of the church's history swept over me as soon as we entered the sanctuary. I was wearing my Santa robe on that day, and I had my favorite set of sleigh bells given to me by a dear friend in one hand and a small candle in a brass holder in the other hand.

Our photographer captured the perfect photo of me standing in front of one of the church windows. When we later saw the finished photographs from our visit to the church, there was a distinct halo around the light of the candle, almost like a divine reflection from above. It became obvious to all of us that the title of this new painting should be *The Light* accompanied by one of my favorite verses: "...let your light shine before others, that they may see your good deeds and glorify your Father in heaven" (Matt. 5:16, NIV).

The Journey

During the same visit to Laurens in 2003, Linda and her photographer and I took a stroll along a riverbank outside of town. As I walked along the quiet bank of the river, alone in the stillness of the moment, I reflected on God's goodness to me, and how He has blessed my ministry. Imagine my surprise when Linda unveiled the 2005 Santa painting depicting me as a shepherd with seven full-grown sheep around my feet. I'm holding a hand-carved staff made by another one of Linda's artistic friends. The seven sheep reminded me of the dreams that Pharaoh had in the Bible. Truly God had me on a journey, as this painting was appropriately named. The verse: "He has shown you, O mortal, what is good. And what does the Lord require of you? To act justly and to love mercy and to walk humbly with your God" (Mic. 6:8, NIV).

Now that I am in my seventh score of years, the significance of the number seven has manifested itself over and over in my life. I can pinpoint significant things that have happened to me every seven years. As I enter my seventieth year of blessings, I like this verse: "And it shall come to pass afterward that I will pour out My Spirit upon all flesh; and your sons and daughters shall prophesy, your old men shall dream dreams, your young men will see visions" (Joel 2:28, KJ21).

The Message

Every Santa portrayer needs his own sleigh! Mine stays in the carport right next to my Santa House. Every year I am honored to man the sleigh in my hometown of High Point, NC in the Christmas parade, and I have also sat in the famous sleigh with a full team of reindeer at the Charles W. Howard Santa Claus School in Midland, MI. However, I have to be honest that I have never piloted a "miniature sleigh with eight tiny reindeer." Linda's 2009 Santa painting shows me piloting my own sleigh in the Christmas Eve sky. The stars in the sky even herald the hope of heaven for "Peace on Earth," the message the angels spread on that first Christmas night and the same message Santa tries to continue to spread over all the world.

The quilt in my lap was made by my grandmother with the help of my great grandmother. It is a crazy quilt fashioned from bits and pieces of clothing worn by my ancestors, and is an heirloom that I treasure. I even took the quilt to my seamstress to have a robe made from it. Her first response was an exclamation of "You're not going to cut that up, are you?!" After I assured her that the quilt had been in storage for over 35 years, and that I would rather wear it as a garment to honor my grandparents, she responded, "Well, we'll have to be a good carpenter and measure twice before we cut."

Now, every time I wear "Santa's Coat of Many Colors," a sense of peace overwhelms me as referenced in the verse that accompanies the prints of the painting: "Now may the God of Peace...that great Shepherd of the sheep, equip you with everything good for doing his will..." (Hebrews 13:20-21, NIV). What an honor it was for me to be able to wear the robe made from my grandmother's crazy quilt that my seamstress made for our next photo session at the same pre-Civil War church in Laurens, SC. Linda asked me to sit in one of the ornate chairs in front of the sanctuary, probably the pastor's chair. I always carry my "Santa's Pocket Watch" with me. As I looked at my watch, the inspiration for this painting was born. It's no coincidence that a beautiful wood carving of *The Last Supper* is behind the chair. It is my belief that one day that we will see Jesus again, but as the scripture says on this print: "You also must be ready, because the Son of Man will come at an hour when you do not expect him" (Luke 12:40, NIV).

The Spirit

I don't want to give away too many secrets, but when I'm not at the North Pole and am at Santa's other home in North Carolina, we don't get much snow! So, when Linda decided she wanted some reference photos of me in the snow, I had to travel to the mountains of North Carolina to find some! The results of my "snow day" came out in 2013 in the painting titled *The Spirit*.

In the painting, Santa is holding a dove, the symbol of the Holy Spirit: "But the fruit of the Spirit is love, joy, peace, forbearance, kindness, goodness, faithfulness..." (Galatians 5:22, NIV). All of these qualities a good Santa should practice, and anyone else for that matter.

Light at the End of the Tunnel